Trust the Process

Trust the God of the Process

Dr. Jim Garrett
Cheri Garrett

take heart books

Trust the Process

Trust the God of the Process

#GarrettLifePrinciples

Published by
Take Heart Books LLC, Toledo, OH
Cover design by Take Heart Books
Artwork by Canva

take heart books

Scripture quotations marked (NIV) are taken from the Holy Bible, New International Version®, NIV®. Copyright © 1973, 1978, 1984, 2011 by Biblica, Inc.™ Used by permission of Zondervan. All rights reserved worldwide. www.zondervan.comThe "NIV" and "New International Version" are trademarks registered in the United States Patent and Trademark Office by Biblica, Inc.™

Scripture quotations marked (AMP) are taken from the Amplified Bible, Copyright © 2015 by The Lockman Foundation. Used by permission.

Scripture quotations marked (AMPCE) are taken from the Amplified Bible, Copyright © 1954, 1958, 1962, 1964, 1965, 1987 by The Lockman Foundation. Used by permission.

Scripture quotations marked (NLT) are taken from the Holy Bible, New Living Translation, copyright ©1996, 2004, 2015 by Tyndale House Foundation. Used by permission of Tyndale House Publishers, Carol Stream, Illinois 60188. All rights reserved.

Scripture quotations from The Authorized (King James) Version. Rights in the Authorized Version in the United Kingdom are vested in the Crown. Reproduced by permission of the Crown's patentee, Cambridge University Press.

Scripture quotations taken from the (NASB®) New American Standard Bible®, Copyright © 1960, 1971, 1977, 1995, 2020 by The Lockman Foundation. Used by permission. All rights reserved. lockman.org

Scripture quotations marked (CEV) are from the Contemporary English Version Copyright © 1991, 1992, 1995 by American Bible Society, Used by Permission.

Scripture taken from the New King James Version®. Copyright © 1982 by Thomas Nelson. Used by permission. All rights reserved.

ISBN: 978-1-958818-08-4 (paperback)

Dedication

As we look at what has passed through our hands, our minds, our hearts, and even our lips when these words were initially spoken, we know that there are individuals who are deserving of our thanksgiving and love.

We recognize that these words were placed in our hearts by the Lord Himself—so we first want to dedicate this work to Him and to His inspiration and anointing.
Lord, we dedicate this book to you.

We want to dedicate this book to the several churches who have allowed us the privilege of being their pastors and preachers in different capacities. Much of this God gave us when we pastored you. You all have been part of this journey and have been used by God to trust us, to bear with us, and even to refine us in our communication of His sovereign Words.
To our Church Families in the past, we dedicate this book to you.

And finally, we want to dedicate this work to our mothers—who both reared us in the nurture and admonition of the Lord, who pointed us in the right direction, and who encouraged us along the way.
Betty Ann Mackey Fricks and Frances Elizabeth Nelson Garrett, we dedicate this book to you.

Contents

Foreword

— 🙶 —

"It is because of their passion, and allowing God to work through them in my life, that I am the husband, the father, the worship leader, and the pastor that I am."

James C. Garrett

MY PRAYER, as I write this short message about Pastors Jim and Cheri Garrett, is that my passion (and love) for them pours into this, just as their passion and love has poured into me and the lives of so many before and after me.

I have had the <u>privilege and honor</u> to be under the ministry leadership of Pastors Jim & Cheri in many different capacities. They were my children's pastors, my youth pastors, my senior pastors, and my parents. My entire life—in my 39 years of being ministered to by them, serving in ministry under their leadership, and ministering beside them—I have watched as my parents ferociously poured into so many different people. It is because of their passion, and allowing God to work through them in my life, that I am the husband, the father, the worship leader, and the pastor that I am today.

I have watched them throughout my life and, as you read this book about *the process* that God takes each of us through, know that I have seen them constantly in the midst of their process. I have watched in the difficult times, I have been with them through many of the highs and lows, and they have remained faithful through it all. In times when many have broken, they have stayed the course with their trust firmly in God. I know this because I was many times the cause of their difficult times. LOL. What they speak on is not simply their take on what the Bible says; instead, it is them taking the Word of God and applying it to each situation they face and watching God work the impossible in their lives. From difficult upbringings, to raising a family of five on a low income, heartbreak in ministry, to triumphs in ministry, and having to defend their children (mainly me) in some difficult times, to watching each of their children and their spouses step into ministry and now, to see grandchildren stepping into God's purpose for their lives...

Pastor Jim (Dad) has always been an innovator in his ministry, coming up with new ways to reach the younger generation and use their talents, hobbies, and desires to show them how to advance God's kingdom. I watched as he led a youth group of 35-40 teenagers and turned it into a group of 500 teenagers. He did not do that by making it games and fun; instead, he did it by teaching God's Word in a way that they could understand and relate to. He not only taught it, but through service, discipleship, and standing next to them in ministry, he showed them how to apply it to their lives.

Pastor Cheri Garrett (Mom) is the heart and passion behind all of it. Her desire to bring people together and fellowship with them is such a beautiful thing to see. She loves so strongly and encourages in all things. The process God has and continues to take her through has led her from a shy, insecure little girl to a world changer. She allows God to use her to will things into existence. She is stubborn (I get it honestly) for the things of God and uses her passion, her fight, and her heart for others to advance the Kingdom of God.

Together, this team has helped—and will continue to help—build an army of history-makers, and I can't wait to see what happens next. Luckily for me, they're my parents, so I get to witness and be a part of it daily, and will continue to watch, learn, and carry on their legacy in all that I do.

Thank you,

Jamie Garrett

Preface

— ❞ —

"Everything from God comes to us through such processes."

Dr. Jim and Cheri Garrett

LIFE SEEMS TO BE REVOLVING AT SUCH A RAPID PACE—yet everything seems to take so long to come to fruition. We often look at life and think that we are in such a fast-paced situation—yet the truth is, we have moved in this direction for so long, and life—even though exponentially "speeding up," still takes time.

Even our microwaves take time anymore—it may be mere seconds—but it takes time, nonetheless.

Time is always a necessity in ALL the processes of our lives.

As you read this book, you will observe various processes and time investments:

- » **Diamonds** are products of time, heat, and pressure.
- » Fine **wines** are products of effort, aging, quality products, and patience.
- » God's creation, *la mariposa* (the butterfly), is the consequence of a brief process known as metamor -phosis, where the humble caterpillar—through a quite "ugly" operation where body tissues break down and reform as wings, legs, and other adult parts until a beautiful butterfly emerges and soars!
- » Jewelry-quality **pearls** are products of months, irritations, and various pressures and works of God.
- » Even **steeping** a quality cup or glass of **tea** is a prescribed process.

In fact, all of these products—and more—are fruit of the inspiration of the Holy Spirit, His plans, and various processes found throughout life. In this aspect, these products are similar to the imago Dei—God's creation: humanity.

Everything from God comes to us through such processes.

His process may seem long-term for us and highly complicated. God works in us through processes. He surrounds us with processes. He shows us how He works in us through the various processes of life.

As you invest your time by reading this book, our prayer is that you will understand more about the world around you, you will sense more about His hand in "nature", and you will seek to cooperate with what the Holy Spirit is working in you.

In this book, we have presented vignettes of God's great work. These are revealed through natural phenomena that most all of us are familiar with. Perhaps, most of us have even read or studied about these things, witnessed these things, partaken in these things, and been amazed by these things.

As you read this, *be challenged* by the Holy Spirit. *Seek* to know Him more and *yield your life* more devotedly to Him and His processes in you.

Trust the Process… **Trust the God of the Process**,
Pastors Jim and Cheri Garrett

The Butterfly Process

Focus on the purpose, not the pain.
God has a purpose for the process you are in.
Know that there is no pain without purpose.

Jim **X** Cheri

THERE IS A STORY TOLD OF A MAN who found a butterfly cocoon.

One day, a small opening appeared. He sat and watched the butterfly for several hours as it struggled to force its body through that little hole. Then it seemed to stop making any progress.

It appeared as if that butterfly had gotten as far as it could and it could go no farther. Then the man decided to help the butterfly, so he took a pair of scissors and snipped off the remaining bit of the cocoon. The butterfly then emerged easily.

But it had a swollen body and small, shriveled wings. The man continued to watch the butterfly because he expected that, at any moment, the wings would enlarge and expand to be able to support the body, which would contract in time.

Neither happened!

In fact, the butterfly spent the rest of its life crawling around with a swollen body and shriveled wings.

It never was able to fly.

What the man, (in his kindness and haste) did not understand, was that the restricting cocoon and the struggle required for the butterfly to get through the tiny opening, were nature's way of forcing fluid from the body of the butterfly into its wings, so that it would be ready for flight once it achieved its freedom from the cocoon. (*Source / author unknown*)

In our own metamorphosis, or transformation, we need the struggle just like the butterfly. It is all part of the process... the process of transforming us into all that He created and purposed us to be.

Always remember that in every stage of the process, God is for you; He is not against you. He loves you! He wants to bless you! He wants you healed, whole, and free; free to be the person He created you to be.

Don't give up in the struggle.
The struggles are just what you need to break free and to be the strong, amazing person that He knew was inside of you since before you ever were—because He is the One who created you!

Part One
The Creation of a Diamond

"For I know the thoughts and plans that I have for you," says the Lord, "thoughts and plans for welfare and peace and not for evil, to give you hope in your final outcome."
Jeremiah 29:11 (AMPCE)

Romans

And we know
that God causes
everything to work
together for the
good

Jim 2 Cheri

8:28 NLT

of those who love God and are called according to his purpose for them.

1

IN 1947'S ACTION COMICS #115, IN THE SUPERMAN STORY called *"The Wish That Came True!,"* Superman (as Clark Kent) is seen squeezing a lump of coal and creating a giant diamond. Although diamonds and coal are both created from carbon under great pressure, such a story is merely a myth due to the purity of the carbon needed for the diamond. Nonetheless, consider the process of carbon being turned into diamonds.

Scientists tell us that diamonds are formed from carbon that has undergone a process requiring great time, great heat, and great pressure. These same scientists tell us that there is a limited amount of space—90 miles beneath the surface of the earth—where this process can take place. Further, they tell us that the process of the formation of diamonds requires a temperature of at least 2,000 degrees Fahrenheit. Then, they also tell us that it takes several million years for diamonds to form. (I don't agree with them on this point because I do not believe the world is nearly that old.)

What I want us to see through all of this is the fact that a diamond, that valuable stone that some consider to be a woman's best friend, comes to us through a process. Notice that this process takes a great length of time, a tremendous amount of heat, and intense pressure--all of this in a LIMITED amount of space HIDDEN deeply beneath the surface of the earth.

Life Principle

Every good thing, like a diamond, comes by means of a process. And the process, which may be painful and time-consuming—and many times in cramped and hidden quarters—is a necessary part in the production of anything of true and lasting value.

Rest assured, as far as God's Kingdom is concerned, you are valuable, more valuable than a diamond, and God wants to take you through the process—His process.

CONSIDER THE BIBLE

ABRAHAM

Biblically, consider for a moment the ancient Patriarch from Ur of the Chaldees, Abraham. God took Abraham through His process. The Bible tells us that although Abraham (initially Abram) was comfortable in his birthland, he stepped out in faith—not knowing what he was going to face or even where he was going.

> *The Lord had said to Abram, "Leave your native country, your relatives, and your father's family, and go to the land that I will show you. I will make you into a great nation. I will bless you and make you famous, and you will be a blessing to others. I will bless those who bless you and curse those who treat you with contempt. All the families on earth will be blessed through you." So Abram departed as the Lord had instructed, and Lot went with him. Abram was seventy-five years old when he left Haran.*
> Genesis 12:1-4 (NLT)

Notice these things about Abraham's adventure:

1. God said "(Abram, you) <u>Go</u>!"
2. God said, "I <u>will</u> show you!"
3. God said, "I <u>will</u> bless you!"
4. God said, "You (Abram) <u>will</u> be a blesssing to others!"

I remember when a time came in our lives that a door shut for us; and no other door was open. We were finally in a place that felt like our dream of God's plan for our lives—where we would finish out our ministry in this place and retire. We were mentoring and preparing young men and women to walk in their gifts and callings and passing on the passion God put in our hearts for the next generation. We were family ministry pastors overseeing family ministries in a large, multi-campus ministry. It was our hearts' calling and desire.

Then the door slammed shut. It was painful. It hurt. We endured rejection. We didn't know what was next.

And God said, *Go. Go to a place I **will** show you.*

We had no idea where or when He would show us. All we knew was that it was time to go. And He said He would bless us. It surely didn't feel like a blessing. And then He said we would be a blessing to others. But, how and when? It didn't happen quickly. It was several years of trusting God **through the process**, as He worked some things out of us and some things in us. It required faith... faith to go... faith to stay... faith to complete the process.

Life Principle

God's process requires faith. Faith to go...faith to stay...and faith to complete the process.
Trust the process. It will bless you and it will bless others.

No Limitations

Notice, too, that Abraham began his adventure at about 75 years of age. *Why is that an important statement?* Because there is not a "too young" or "too old" age to begin your adventure. There is not a "too anything" in order to start being used by God. The limits we place on being used by God are limits that are artificial, or at least, merely conceived in our own minds; they are not God-imposed limitations. Notice, too, that when God spoke to Abram to begin the process of becoming a great nation, he (Abram) had no children and Sarai, his wife, was barren. But God's process doesn't recognize our human limitations; eventually, Abram became Abraham and fathered his chosen son when he was 100 years old. (His wife was 90!)

Life Principle

The process has NOTHING to do with age or any human set limitations. It is all about preparing us—maturing us—completing us.
Trust the process.

Jim and I were watching a music awards television show one night and they were honoring all the musicians that paved the way for the younger generation of musicians.

It was so moving. We thought about how, in the church world, it had become all about the young generation without regard to those who paved the way before them. It often appears that they didn't need the experience and mentorship of those who have given it all for God's call (or as it is called in the music industry, "those who had paid their dues").

As we started ministry, there was no "package." We actually started volunteering as youth pastors and worship leaders. There was no life insurance or retirement plan. There was only passion and calling. And that is what needs to be passed on to the next generation. (Perhaps with a bit more wisdom than we had, BUT, it needs to be passed on nonetheless.)

We began to wonder why, in the church world, we don't seem to appreciate and celebrate those who paved the way for us; instead, we push them to the side. We MUST REMEMBER that the process has nothing to do with age or human-set limitations. The process is preparing us at every age for what God has next for us—and for Him. God has prepared us to help make ready and help others along in their process of maturation and completion.

As in each process that all of God's servants go through, Abraham's faith was tested by the sacrifice of his only son at that time, born to Sarai—Isaac. (Genesis 22) This was part of God's process in Abraham. Like the pressures needed to create a diamond, ALL of God's processes ALWAYS contain pressures of some kind. At least to us, we know these as *pressures*: tests, trials, and all sorts of other things. And these pressures are painful, but necessary, for God's work to be completed in us—and I assure you that God's work which He has "begun" in you will be brought to be a "completed" work in you.

Jim **8** Cheri

Philippians 1:6 reminds us, *And I am certain that God, who began the good work within you, will continue his work until it is finally finished on the day when Christ Jesus returns.* (NLT)

Be reminded of three things:

1. God's process ALWAYS requries obedience and sacrifice.
2. The process always requires testing.
3. The process will be painful—but God's end result will be worth it—for the Kindgom of God—and for you and me.

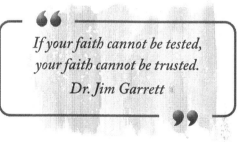

> *If your faith cannot be tested,*
> *your faith cannot be trusted.*
> Dr. Jim Garrett

Life Principle

God's process may require us to sacrifice the very thing we believe to be our answer—the way to His blessing. But remember, *Trust the process.*

God required us to sacrifice our dream, where we believed God called us, for a time in the desert, the wilderness. To go—not knowing where or what that meant. It was part of our process.

Abraham was faithful to complete the process, and he walked out his purpose and was blessed by God. He truly did become the father of many peoples! And he was a very financially (and otherwise) prosperous man. And he did become a blessing to the entire world. In fact, his blessing continues to reach the world today. Did you know that more inventions and achievements per capita that have been for the good of the world have come out of one branch of Abraham's descendants—Israel?

And know this, as well: You, too, will be better because of God's process. Although not in the same way as Abraham, know that you, too, will be used of God to bless His world.

Life Principle

> Stay in the process, obedient and faithful. You will see how God will use the process to prepare you and to use you and to mature you and to complete you. *Trust the process.*

Through God's process in Abraham, His plan prospered. And God's plan for you will prosper in the process—both His Kingdom plan and His personal plan for you.

Life Principle

> The diamond is a very beautiful stone. It requires much time, intense heat, and great pressure. And its worth is valued by all, not just those who shop at jewelers. As a small stone is valued only after it has passed through the long time, extreme pressure, and intense heat, so, too, our true value is revealed in us—only after the time, the pressure, and the heat of the process.
> *Trust the process.*

Process Comes in Waves

This part of our process was several years long. Finding ways to make ends meet while we waited, being faithful where God planted us while we waited. We endured the time, the intense heat, and the great pressure. It wasn't fun. There were days we just didn't understand. The financial pressure was so difficult. The living situation was very humbling. *But God was using it all to mine the diamond He had designed on the inside of us.* We had to remind ourselves (and each other) to trust the process—and more importantly, to *trust the God of the process.*

And so, a Biblical truth is now revealed: **God takes His children <u>through</u> the process.**

Shadrach, Meshach, and Abednego

One Bible story is that of Daniel's three Hebrew friends who faced the process. We know them as Shadrach, Meshach, and Abednego.

Look at what the Bible tells us about them:

- **Daniel 1:6,** "Daniel, Hananiah, Mishael, and Azariah were four of the young men chosen, all from the tribe of Judah." (NLT)
- **Daniel 1:19-20,** "The king talked with them, and no one impressed him as much as Daniel, Hananiah, Mishael, and Azariah. So they entered the royal service. Whenever the king consulted them in any matter requiring wisdom and balanced judgment, he found them ten times more capable than any of the magicians and enchanters in his entire kingdom." (NLT)

Yet their lives were extremely uncomfortable. Their captors, associates, and fellow servants laid an accurate, but deathly, accusation against them; they simply would not obey the king by observing his command to bow before the king's golden image. Of course, you know these latter three men as Shadrach, Meshach, and Abednego.

- **Daniel 3:12,** "But there are some Jews—Shadrach, Meshach, and Abednego—whom you have put in charge of the province of Babylon. They pay no attention to you, Your Majesty. They refuse to serve your gods and do not worship the gold statue you have set up." (NLT)
- **Daniel 3:14,** Nebuchadnezzar said to them, "Is it true, Shadrach, Meshach, and Abednego, that you refuse to serve my gods or to worship the gold statue I have set up?" (NLT)
- **Daniel 3:16-17,** Shadrach, Meshach, and Abednego replied, "O Nebuchadnezzar, we do not need to defend ourselves before you. [17] If we are thrown into the blazing furnace, the God whom we serve is able to save us. He will rescue us from your power, Your Majesty. (NLT)

The three Hebrew children remind us that sometimes God's process for us is uncomfortable heat like it takes to form a diamond. *Trust the process.*

But let's move on: These young men were willing to die in the process.

- **Daniel 3:18,** "But even if he doesn't, we want to make it clear to you, Your Majesty, that we will never serve your gods or worship the gold statue you have set up."(NLT)

So you see, **dying to self is part of the process.** We must trust the process—even as Shadrach, Meshach, and Abednego did. And in their lives, God's plan prospered in the end.

- Daniel 3:24-25,28-29, But suddenly, Nebuchadnezzar jumped up in amazement and exclaimed to his advisers, "Didn't we tie up three men and throw them into the furnace?" "Yes, Your Majesty, we certainly did," they replied. "Look!" Nebuchadnezzar shouted. "I see four men, unbound, walking around in the fire unharmed! And the fourth looks like a god!" Then Nebuchadnezzar said, "Praise to the God of Shadrach, Meshach, and Abednego! He sent his angel to rescue his servants who trusted in him. They defied the king's command and were willing to die rather than serve or worship any god except their own God. Therefore, I make this decree: If any people, whatever their race or nation or language, speak a word against the God of Shadrach, Meshach, and Abednego, they will be torn limb from limb, and their houses will be turned into heaps of rubble. There is no other god who can rescue like this!" (NLT)

God was right in the middle of the fire with them. After the process came to completion, the three Hebrew children prospered in the end, as did God's entire plan and Kingdom.

- Daniel 3:30, Then the king promoted Shadrach, Meshach, and Abednego to even higher positions in the province of Babylon. (NLT)

God will never leave you in the process alone. He is right there in the fire with you.

JOB

Job also faced the process.

- **Job 1:8,** Then the LORD asked Satan, "Have you noticed my servant Job? He is the finest man in all the earth. He is blameless—a man of complete integrity. He fears God and stays away from evil." (NLT)

Job's process became a particularly uncomfortable one.

- **Job 1:12 (NLT),** "All right, you may test him," the LORD said to Satan. "Do whatever you want with everything he possesses, but don't harm him physically." So Satan left the LORD's presence. (NLT)

And Job was so intent on serving God that he was even willing to die in the process.

- **Job 13:15,** Though he slay me, yet will I hope in him; I will surely defend my ways to his face. (NIV)

But then again—as did Abraham, as did the three Hebrew children—the Kingdom of God prospered in the end, as Job prospered in the end, and, *as you, too,* can prosper when the process completes its work in you.

- **Job 42:10,** After Job had prayed for his friends, the LORD restored his fortunes and gave him twice as much as he had before. (NIV)

Trust God to restore and prosper you through the process. He is mining for the diamond he sees in you.

JOHN THE DISCIPLE

Consider for a moment one of Jesus' closest followers, the one called the Beloved, John the disciple. He also faced the process. It, too, was an uncomfortable process. Historians tell us that he was boiled in oil. He was later exiled to a prison island named Patmos. And through the process, God's Word, written by the hand of this "man in process," went out to the Kingdom of God. And it is still enlarging the Kingdom of God today.

Have you ever heard of the Gospel according to John or the Book of Revelation? Some reliable theologians and historians say this same John wrote 1, 2, and 3 John, as well. The important fact is that through this John, this "man in process," the Kingdom of God was extended and is <u>still</u> being extended.

Life Principle

The process is uncomfortable. Some kind of dying will go on in the process, but it is working in you something great. *Choose to stay in the process.*

So truly, the process is always for His good; and for our good, as well. Again, we like to remember that passage in Jeremiah 29:11, *"For I know the plans I have for you,"* says the LORD. *"They are plans for good and not for disaster, to give you a future and a hope."* (NLT)

We, too, either are facing the process, or right in the middle of it. And it will, in all probability, be an uncomfortable process; a painful process. Remember the pressures of the creation of a diamond? There may even be a sense of "death" in the process. But we should remember those famous words of Job 13:15, *"Though he slay me, yet will __I hope in him__; I will surely defend my ways to his face."* (NIV) (emphasis added)

After death, there is life—there is transformation in the process. And we will prosper in the end—as will His Kingdom.

And we know that God causes everything to work together for the good of those who love God and are called according to his purpose for them.
Romans 8:28 (NLT)

Life Principle

The process is preparing you:
Maturing you. Completing you. You see yourself as that piece of coal / carbon, but God sees the diamond He created you to be—and He is after that diamond.
Friends, *Trust the process!*

Part Two
The Process of Winemaking

O Lᴏʀᴅ my God, you have performed many wonders for us.
Your plans for us are too numerous to list.
Psalm 40:5a (NLT)

Don't copy the behavior and customs of this world, but let God transform you into a new person by changing the way you think.

Romans

12:2 *NLT*

Then you will
learn to know
God's will for you,
which is good and
pleasing and
perfect.

2

I HAVE NEVER BEEN ONE WHO DRANK WINE. My medical doctor once suggested to me that I should drink wine because of the benefits it would have toward heart healthiness. But there was a problem: I didn't like the taste of it. Nonetheless, I understand that there are individuals who fancy a good wine here in the United States of America, and that there are countries where wine flows even as water flows. So, I did a little research on the process of making wine.

I found out that winemaking is a several-stage process. First, I found out that there is a science to choosing **the proper location to grow the grape vines,** there are **proper soils** to grow the plants in, and **there are the proper plants** themselves for growing the quality fruit. For new growths, this takes a lot of research and experimentation. For tougher, older, established vineyards, many of them simply continue doing what has worked for their families and friends for centuries.

After all has been chosen and after the fruit has grown, then comes the **harvesting of the fruit.** For my example here, I have chosen grapes since that seems to be the most common fruit for fine wines. Rest assured that for fine wines, **only the best fruits are chosen.** This is only natural because vineyards have a reputation to uphold. Of course, they choose their best.

All of this takes time in the choosing and experimenting process. And for this, the crucial element IS the time factor. One does not want to rush through the process and find an inferior method or product; otherwise, this entire aspect of the process will have to be redone until proper and desired results are found.

But then comes another crucial element: a series of crushings / pressings. These are often done by machines, or, as in some places such as France for certain types of wine, these pressings come by stomping with the feet. I can remember as a little child watching an episode of *I Love Lucy* on our old, black and white television, where she was stomping in a vat of grapes. Oh, the faces Lucy made while she was doing this! Well, it made for good TV entertainment back then, but—it is a reality today of the process of making wine in some countries. And I don't know if grapes have feelings. (I suspect they don't, but I am told by some authors that plants DO indeed have feelings.) But if grapes DO have feelings, I am pretty sure this process is not fun for them, either. In fact, this process produces a CRUSHING and a DYING on the part of the grape. But it is all a necessary part of the process.

I am reminded of one of my favorite places in Jerusalem that was very dear to Jesus. It is called the Garden of Gethsemane. The word, Gethsemane, means "pressing" or "crushing." You might even think of the terms, "squeezing" or "pressuring" place where olives are crushed to produce olive oil.

I think that when Jesus was crying great tears of blood in that garden, there was a great pressuring taking place within Him. I know that His agony then, and shortly thereafter, was beyond my imagination BUT, I can fathom the idea of the weight His heart was under—but only as an inkling of the real pressure He was under.

Next comes a **fermentation** process in which, over time, the sugars in the juice are transformed into alcohol. Obviously, I am not going to try to explain that which I do not understand myself, but somehow, sugars, within the grapes and their juices, go through a time process and are transformed into alcohol. I am pretty sure a good high school chemistry student could explain this transformation, BUT I want to make a point here. I DO NOT understand this process. I do not grasp what is taking place. *But did you know that my understanding is not a factor in this process?* **The process continues whether I know what is going on or not.** (In fact, it continues whether I like it or not, it continues whether I see it or not, it continues whether it feels good or not.)

Life Principle

My understanding is not a necessary ingredient in God's process. This little fact can change our entire perception of what God is doing within us. We do NOT have to understand what we are going through.
The necessary ingredient is trust. Trust the process.

- After a first series of transformations, there is a secondary transformation into which the wine-to-be is further changed. The aging process... time.
- This both decreases the acidity of the wine AND it softens the flavor.
- This again takes time and, in the process, filters off, settles, and clarifies the wine.
- The amount of time taken to transform the wine can be from a few months to more than 20 years.
- The process starts with a choice. Our process started when God chose us as His very own, and when we responded to

His choice by receiving Him.
- Then, there are pressings and crushings that change us.
- And then, there is time. The process in us takes time.

Even as [in His love] He chose us [actually picked us out for Himself as His own] in Christ before the foundation of the world, that we should be holy (consecrated and set apart for Him) and blameless in His sight, even above reproach, before Him in love.
Ephesians 1:4 (AMPCE)

And the winemaking process ends when a delightful and healthy beverage is brought forth to the table to be useful and to be enjoyed. The process in us makes us more like Jesus and prepares us for His purpose and plan.

MOSES

Another Biblical look at the process God brings us through is found in the life of Moses.

What we will see here, are the *early stages of the process.* They are true in the process of making wine, they were true in the life of Moses, and they are true in our lives.

Even as is seen early in one's faith, in the process of making wine, we see that a growing and harvesting of the fruit must take place. In other words, there has to be something to make the wine out of. During this time, there is great care given to the vines so that they can produce excellent fruit. One might even say that these vines are pampered by the great care given to them. I believe this is a great picture of the visible, manifest grace that is shown to many of us when we come to Christ and walk as "babes" in Him. His grace remains with us all throughout our Christian lives. But this is a time of tangible grace when we don't have a capacity to even know HOW to grow in Him.

And it is Jesus Himself Who uses the illustration of us—the branches—being attached to Him, the Vine.

> *"Yes, I am the vine; you are the branches. Those who remain in me, and I in them, will produce much fruit. For apart from me you can do nothing."*
> **John 15:5 (NLT)**

So, we are calling this time of early Christian birth a "Growing on the vine—a time of extreme grace." This is a time of "overlooking" things, for pampering certain aspects, all for the sake of allowing room for growth.

With Moses, there was a grace that saved him, nurtured him, and trained him during the early part of his process.

You see, Moses was preserved from death.

Exodus 1:22; 2:2-6 tells us,

> *Then Pharaoh gave this order to all his people: "Throw every newborn Hebrew boy into the Nile River. But you may let the girls live." [A Hebrew] woman became pregnant and gave birth to a son. She saw that he was a special baby and kept him hidden for three months. But when she could no longer hide him, she got a basket made of papyrus reeds and waterproofed it with tar and pitch. She put the baby in the basket and laid it among the reeds along the bank of the Nile River. The baby's sister then stood at a distance, watching to see what would*

happen to him. Soon Pharaoh's daughter came down to bathe in the river, and her attendants walked along the riverbank. When the princess saw the basket among the reeds, she sent her maid to get it for her. When the princess opened it, she saw the baby. The little boy was crying, and she felt sorry for him. "This must be one of the Hebrew children," she said.

Exodus 1:22; 2:2-6 (NLT)

Life Principle

Sometimes in the process, God keeps us in a hidden place until the time is right and the preparation is completed. Trust His process.

Later, when the boy was older, his mother brought him back to Pharaoh's daughter, who adopted him as her own son. The princess named him Moses, for she explained, 'I lifted him out of the water.'

Exodus 2:10 (NLT)

And in this process, Moses ended up being nurtured in the house of Pharaoh. Notice indeed, that Moses was found and raised by Pharaoh's own daughter. This certainly included not only kingly nurturing but kingly training as well. By default, it had to. This meant that Moses was trained by the same teachers that taught the children of the Pharaoh.

Life Principle

In the process, God places the right people, with the right heart, in the very center of your life. Trust His process.

PROCESSING ON THE BACK SIDE OF THE DESERT

Moses later found himself being processed on the back side of the desert.

> *Many years later, when Moses had grown up, he went out*
> *to visit his own people, the Hebrews, and he saw how hard*
> *they were forced to work. During his visit, he saw an Egyp-*
> *tian beating one of his fellow Hebrews. After looking in all*
> *directions to make sure no one was watching, Moses killed the*
> *Egyptian and hid the body in the sand. The next day, when*
> *Moses went out to visit his people again, he saw two Hebrew*
> *men fighting. "Why are you beating up your friend?" Moses*
> *said to the one who had started the fight. The man replied,*
> *"Who appointed you to be our prince and judge? Are you going*
> *to kill me as you killed that Egyptian yesterday?" Then Moses*
> *was afraid, thinking, 'Everyone knows what I did.' And sure*
> *enough, Pharaoh heard what had happened, and he tried to*
> *kill Moses. But Moses fled from Pharaoh and went to live in*
> *the land of Midian.*
> Exodus 2:11-15 (NLT)

There are a couple things we need to point out here: Moses was not banished to this desert place. Instead, he fled there because he had exceeded his allowances, limits as a non-Egyptian in the house of the pharaoh, and also, he murdered an Egyptian. He had pushed too far. Many times, as we are being processed, we find ourselves in a place where we feel that we are on the back side of the desert—whether we put ourselves there or whether God had placed us there.

Life Principle

The process, many times, takes us to the backside of the desert where there is no interference with what God is working out in us. *Trust the process* in your desert times.

Note, too, that there was, and is, an uncertainty and a toughness found on the backside of the desert. Moses showed us this because he hadn't planned to be in the place he found himself; it definitely was not in his agenda. Yet, necessity caused him to be there. And because this wasn't in his agenda, Moses had no plans; he was simply taking things as they came and he was dealing with them as they came up.

"An Egyptian rescued us from the shepherds," they answered.
"And then he drew water for us and watered our flocks."
"Then where is he?" their father asked. "Why did you leave
him there? Invite him to come and eat with us."
Moses accepted the invitation, and he settled there with him.
In time, Reuel gave Moses his daughter Zipporah to be his
wife. Later she gave birth to a son, and Moses named him
Gershom, for he explained, "I have been
a foreigner in a foreign land."
Exodus 2:19-22 (NLT)

You might could even call Moses' time in the desert a "pressing" similar to the event that the grapes go through in the preparation of wine—preparation for His purpose.

Life Principle

Crushings and pressings are part of the process. Their purpose is to bring out "stuff" from inside of us that keeps our hearts impure so that the process can transform us to be more like Him. *Trust the process.*

There was much time spent in the desert place, even as the months and years of time are spent in the preparation of wine. In Moses' case, he spent 40 years in that desert place. And note that there were experiences in the desert with God that produced transformation.

THE BURNING BUSH

There the angel of the Lord appeared to him in a blazing fire from the middle of a bush. Moses stared in amazement. Though the bush was engulfed in flames, it didn't burn up. "This is amazing," Moses said to himself. "Why isn't that bush burning up? I must go see it."
When the Lord saw Moses coming to take a closer look, God called to him from the middle of the bush, "Moses! Moses!"
"Here I am!" Moses replied.
"Do not come any closer," the Lord warned. "Take off your sandals, for you are standing on holy ground. I am the God of your father—the God of Abraham, the God of Isaac, and the God of Jacob." When Moses heard this, he covered his face because he was afraid to look at God.
Now go, for I am sending you to Pharaoh. You must lead my people Israel out of Egypt."
Exodus 3:2-6, 10 (NLT)

Jim **28** Cheri

And like some of us, in Moses' life, there was doubt regarding this person—who he was / who we are.

But Moses protested to God, "Who am I to appear before Pharaoh?
Who am I to lead the people of Israel out of Egypt?"
Exodus 3:11 (NLT)

Life Principle

Sometimes in the process we doubt ourselves. We see our shortcomings... our failures... our sins. God wants us to see ourselves as He sees us. He wants us to see that we are never alone. He is right in the middle of the process with us. Trust His process.

Like some of us often do, Moses showed doubt concerning even *Who* was sending him. In a way, again like many of us from time to time, Moses was questioning God.

I'm not so much questioning Moses' doubt, as I am noting that it is so much easier to be and do something when you know *Who* is sending you to do that something and *why* you are doing it in the first place.

But Moses protested, "If I go to the people of Israel and tell
them, 'The God of your ancestors has sent me to you,' they will
ask me, 'What is his name?' Then what should I tell them?"
God replied to Moses, "I AM WHO I AM. Say this to the people of
Israel: I AM has sent me to you." God also said to Moses, "Say
this to the people of Israel: Yahweh, the God of your ancestors—
the God of Abraham, the God of Isaac, and the God of Jacob—
has sent me to you.
Exodus 3:13-15 (NLT)

After being shown whom he was serving in more detail, Moses still showed doubt concerning the full power of the Lord with which he was to lead the Israelites out of Egypt.

But Moses protested again, "What if they won't believe me or listen to me? What if they say,
'The LORD never appeared to you'?"
Then the LORD asked him, "What is that in your hand?"
"A shepherd's staff," Moses replied.
"Throw it down on the ground," the LORD told him. So Moses threw down the staff, and it turned into a snake!
Moses jumped back.
Then the LORD told him, "Reach out and grab its tail." So Moses reached out and grabbed it, and it turned back into a shepherd's staff in his hand. "Perform this sign," the LORD told him. "Then they will believe that the LORD, the God of their ancestors—the God of Abraham, the God of Isaac, and the God of Jacob—really has appeared to you."
Exodus 4:1-5 (NLT)

And then, Moses began to show his hesitations; he even had doubts concerning his abilities.

But Moses pleaded with the LORD, "O Lord, I'm not very good with words. I never have been, and I'm not now, even though you have spoken to me.
I get tongue-tied, and my words get tangled."
Then the LORD asked Moses, "Who makes a person's mouth? Who decides whether people speak or do not speak, hear or do

not hear, see or do not see? Is it not I, the LORD? Now go!
I will be with you as you speak, and I will instruct
you in what to say."
But Moses again pleaded, "Lord, please! Send anyone else."
Then the LORD became angry with Moses.
Exodus 4:10-14 (NLT)

Life Principle

Sometimes in the process, we push God to anger and we
might never see what could have been if we would have
just trusted the process. We must stay in the process.

Moses finally yielded to the process he was going through
and continued further in God's process with him.

So Moses went back home to Jethro, his father-in-law. "Please
let me return to my relatives in Egypt," Moses said. "I don't
even know if they are still alive." "Go in peace," Jethro replied.
Exodus 4:18 (NLT)

We must understand that God's purpose in the process in Moses
was to bring him to a place of deeper *use-ability.*

God wants to do so much through us, but we often attempt
to limit Him because of our doubt, because of our short-comings,
because of our refusal. But we have to remember that *we are in a*
process. He is still working on, and in us. The greatest gifts that we
can offer Him are not our abilities—but, as one author said well,
it is "our availability."

Life Principle

The process will put us in places and before people that will mature our faith in God. The process will require us to do things that others may deem as crazy. Trust the process.

Keep in mind, it wasn't that Moses did not possess some skills before his experience on the back side of the desert. It really wasn't even that Moses was rebellious to God's purpose in him—hesitant, yes—rebellious, no.

Instead, God was simply doing some further perfecting in Moses to prepare him even deeper for the task. Sometimes, it seems that the bigger the task that God has for us, the deeper and longer the preparation and process that are required of us. I suppose there is great reality in that idea. God is preparing us for the plan he has for us.

Life Principle

The process of pressing, crushing and time is working to sweeten you...to filter off and filter out those things that keep you from being more like Him...to settle you in who you are in Him...to clarify in you His purposes and His plans. The process is transforming.
Trust the process.

And, as I said earlier, there is a secondary transformation into which the wine-to-be is further changed. This both decreases the acidity of the wine AND softens the flavor.

Life Principle

Does that remind you of the process in our own lives when God works within us to make us more like Him? Galatians 5 gives us a wonderful reminder of the work that God, by His Holy Spirit, desires to do in every believer. Trust Him in the process.

But the Holy Spirit produces this kind of fruit in our lives: love, joy, peace, patience, kindness, goodness, faithfulness, gentleness, and self-control. There is no law against these things!
Those who belong to Christ Jesus have nailed the passions and desires of their sinful nature to his cross and crucified them there. Since we are living by the Spirit, let us follow the Spirit's leading in every part of our lives. Let us not become conceited, or provoke one another, or be jealous of one another.
Galatians 5:22-26 (NLT)

In the midst of the process, God will send people to you to give you wisdom for the process. The story picks back up in Exodus as God perfects Moses a little bit more—this time through his father-in-law, Jethro.

"This is not good!" Moses' father-in-law exclaimed. "You're going to wear yourself out—and the people, too. This job is too heavy a burden for you to handle all by yourself. Now listen to me, and let me give you a word of advice, and may God be with you. You should continue to be the people's representative before God, bringing their disputes to him.
Exodus 18:17-19 (NLT)

But there also will always be people in the process who are exasperating: Complainers... negative... immature. But we need to realize that in this process, God also uses them to change you. Again, it may be uncomfortable, it may be exasperating and it may be downright obnoxious, but they are necessary for the work God is doing in you.

Then Moses cried out to the Lord, "What should I do with these
people? They are ready to stone me!"
Exodus 17:4 (NLT)

THE DESTINATION... SORT OF
OR AT LEAST—THE FULLFILLMENT OF PURPOSE

The purpose in wine is to be processed, to be drunk and to be enjoyed.

Moses was processed in order to lead the children of Israel out of Egypt and into the Promised Land.

What are you being processed for?

I don't know the response to this dangling statement; only God knows fully. Nonetheless, there is a scriptural word for this thing that we call the "process." That word is *sanctification.*

God has united you with Christ Jesus. For our benefit God
made him to be wisdom itself. Christ made us right with God;
he made us pure and holy, and he freed us from sin.
1 Corinthians 1:30 (NLT)

This is a Greek word in the Bible, *hagiosmos*, that is generally translated as "sanctification" or "pure and holy." But we should quickly take note that this translation only shows part of the real meaning. *Hagiosmos* further means "to be set apart for an appointed service or use." In other words, you and I were never intended to be simple show pieces of God's handiwork. (Although, we are that as well!) Instead, we are God's chosen vessels with God's designated purpose.

> *For I know the plans I have for you," says the LORD. "They*
> *are plans for good and not for disaster, to give you*
> *a future and a hope.*
> Jeremiah 29:11 (NLT)

God definitively has a plan and purpose for you and for me. The process is preparing us for His plan and purpose.

Life Principle

> The process takes time. The time depends much on how we respond to the process, our submission to the process and the transformation it is producing in us. *Trust the process. Trust the God of the process.*

> *Don't copy the behavior and customs of this world, but let God*
> *transform you into a new person by changing the way you*
> *think. Then you will learn to know God's will for you, which is*
> *good and pleasing and perfect.*
> Romans 12:2 (NLT)

Part Three
The Process of Steeping Tea

Commit your actions to the LORD, and your plans will succeed.
Proverbs 16:3 (NLT)

Isaiah

For just as the
heavens are
higher than the
earth,

55:9 NLT

so my ways are
higher than
your ways
and my thoughts
higher than your
thoughts.

3

ONE OF THE THINGS THAT CHERI AND I (and many others) love so much is drinking a tall, ice-cold glass of sweet tea. But did you know that even making tea is considered to be a process?

Steeping tea is the soaking in water of tea leaves, so as to extract the flavors from those leaves. Some teas are prepared for drinking by steeping the leaves, or tea bags, in heated water to release the flavor and nutrients. The desired effect is to draw out those rich tastes of the tea leaves—bagged or loose—in order to produce an excellent and tasty beverage for the enjoyment of self, family, and friends.

With tea, there is first a selection of tea leaves or tea bags. There are many different types of teas and each type must be handled differently to draw out the individual tea's best flavor. Once you have some experience with teas you will be able to recognize the tea by its smell and what it looks like... it doesn't even have to be labeled.

Next, there is a placing of the teabags into boiling water.

Third, there is a "testing" that needs to take place to see how intense the flavor and how the color of the tea now appears.

Following, there is a combination of the tea leaf, the boiling water, and perhaps a sweetening substance. Things like sugar, milk, or lemon can be added to the tea to give it a different taste... not necessarily better, but different.

Then, there might come a filling where additional water or some other substance is added to the tea.

And finally, there is an enjoyment of the product.

Each tea has its perfect steeping conditions... the best temperature to steep it and the perfect amount of time... these conditions produce the best teas.

Factors that contribute to a perfect cup of tea:

- The quality of the tea leaves
- Purity of the water
- Ration of tea to water
- Correct steeping temperature for the specific type of tea
- Correct steeping time for the specific type of tea
- Adequate room for the tea leaves to expand and fully extract the best flavor

Many teas can be re-steeped multiple times.
The tea becomes stronger the longer it is steeped.

JOSEPH

We can see a similar process in the book of Genesis in the life of Joseph. (You know, the one with the *Technicolor Dream Coat*.)

Genesis tells us that Joseph was greatly loved by his father. This sounds all good and wonderful—but remember, where

someone is deeply loved, they are simultaneously deeply hated by those who are often neglected or shunned. That same
thing was going on in Joseph's life.

*Jacob loved Joseph more than any of his other children because
Joseph had been born to him in his old age. So one day Jacob
had a special gift made for Joseph—a beautiful robe. But his
brothers hated Joseph because their father loved him more than
the rest of them. They couldn't say a kind word to him.*
Genesis 37:3-4 (NLT)

And can I say that each of us is also greatly loved of our
Heavenly Father.

Life Principle

There are times in the process when God's favor in our life
causes others to be jealous of us and to say unkind things
to us and about us. They may even hate us. Rather than
anger us or cause us to have bitterness, instead, allow this
part of the process to refine us. God will use the process to
teach us to love our enemies... to forgive them... to pray for
them... and to bless them. Trust the process.

Joseph was also someone who was given to dreams. I think
all of us like to dream—to have hopes for the future and to
develop big plans—and many of those dreams are often much
bigger than we are. And some of them even come from God
Himself.

One night Joseph had a dream, and when he told his brothers
about it, they hated him more than ever.
Genesis 37:5 (NLT)

According to that passage, it seems like God had chosen Joseph early in the process. Sometimes in our process, God may give us pictures of our destiny, too. And He may plant dreams within our spirits. But unlike Joseph, we must be wise in what we should share, and what we should keep to ourselves. We must also be wise concerning with whom we share these things and the right times to share. Because of this, Joseph was hated by his brothers because of his father's love for him, and because of God's apparent use of him and His plans for him.

And we have to ask the question: *Did Joseph possibly share his dream prematurely... possibly even pride-fully... bringing about an intensified time of processing?*

Because of this, Joseph went through a time of extreme *heat*... even a time nearly inflicting death upon him.

So when Joseph arrived, his brothers ripped off the beautiful
robe he was wearing. Then they grabbed him and threw him
into the cistern. Now the cistern was empty; there was no
water in it. Then, just as they were sitting down to eat, they
looked up and saw a caravan of camels in the distance coming
toward them. It was a group of Ishmaelite traders taking a load
of gum, balm, and aromatic resin from Gilead down to Egypt.
Judah said to his brothers, "What will we gain by killing our
brother? We'd have to cover up the crime. Instead of hurting
him, let's sell him to those Ishmaelite traders. After all, he is our
brother—our own flesh and blood!" And his brothers agreed.

So when the Ishmaelites, who were Midianite traders, came
by, Joseph's brothers pulled him out of the cistern and sold him
to them for twenty pieces of silver.
And the traders took him to Egypt.
Genesis 37:23-28 (NLT)

Life Principle

Sometimes in the process, we are sold out by those who are jealous, insecure or filled with hate. This is most painful when it is those who are the closest to us. In times like these, we must trust the heart of the God of the process. He can, and will, take the good, the bad, the beautiful, and the ugly and work it all together for our good and for His glory.
But trust the process.

In Joseph's life, God's choice of him became even more apparent.

Meanwhile, the Midianite traders arrived in Egypt, where
they sold Joseph to Potiphar, an officer of Pharaoh,
the king of Egypt.
Potiphar was captain of the palace guard.
Genesis 37:36 (NLT)

In fact, God's handiwork in Joseph became increasingly obvious to all who were around him.

The Lord was with Joseph, so he succeeded in everything he
did as he served in the home of his Egyptian master. Potiphar
noticed this and realized that the Lord was with Joseph, giving
him success in everything he did. This pleased Potiphar, so he

soon made Joseph his personal attendant. He put him in charge of his entire household and everything he owned. From the day Joseph was put in charge of his master's household and property, the Lord began to bless Potiphar's household for Joseph's sake. All his household affairs ran smoothly, and his crops and livestock flourished. So Potiphar gave Joseph complete administrative responsibility over everything he owned. With Joseph there, he didn't worry about a thing—except what kind of food to eat!

Genesis 39:2-6 (NLT)

Life Principle

Even when we find ourselves in a place that is uncomfortable...a place where we don't want to be...a place where we question God's purpose and plan for our lives... as we remain faithful with our gifts, and as we remain faithful as His servants—we can see God bless us and we can see Him bless what we do and bless others through us.
Always trust the process.

And, as is often the case in our lives, the heat was turned even hotter upon Joseph: this time, again, because of the character and qualities that he possessed. And then, I am reminded that when one is steeping a tea, the heat must burn a little stronger and a little longer in order to produce the strength of product that the maker is looking for.

And Joseph's preparation wasn't over yet. The next thing that happened to him was that he was seduced by Potiphar's wife.

Joseph was a very handsome and well-built young man, and Potiphar's wife soon began to look at him lustfully. "Come and sleep with me," she demanded. But Joseph refused. "Look," he told her, "my master trusts me with everything in his entire household. No one here has more authority than I do. He has held back nothing from me except you, because you are his wife. How could I do such a wicked thing? It would be a great sin against God."
Genesis 39:6b-9 (NLT)

Life Principle

In the midst of the process, there will be frequent tests of our character and integrity. Trust the process.

Through no fault of his own, other than his good-looks and other appealing characteristics, Joseph found himself being tested. And unfortunately (or so it seemed), others believed the false accusations against Joseph. In this case, it certainly seems as if more fuel was being poured on the fire when Potiphar's wife claimed Joseph raped her.

Potiphar was furious when he heard his wife's story about how Joseph had treated her. So he took Joseph and threw him into the prison where the king's prisoners were held, and there he remained.
Genesis 39:19-20 (NLT)

Remember what I said earlier? *The tea becomes stronger the longer it is steeped.*

Life Principle

Sometimes in the process, the heat gets much hotter before that process produces what God is looking for.
Trust the God of the process.

When we remain in the character that God has been forming within us, His pleasure is manifest in His keeping and exalting of us. This is perhaps similar to God's sweetener being poured upon us as our tea leaves steep.

But the Lord was with Joseph in the prison and showed him his faithful love. And the Lord made Joseph a favorite with the prison warden. Before long, the warden put Joseph in charge of all the other prisoners and over everything that happened in the prison. The warden had no more worries, because Joseph took care of everything. The Lord was with him and caused everything he did to succeed.
Genesis 39:21-23 (NLT)

Life Principle

God can cause us to receive favor even when the process is like a prison with all the doors shut and locked and barred. He can increase us and cause us to succeed in the worst of situations. Trust Him in the process.

God uses those who trust in Him. Even in the process, God uses us and our gifts in the lives of others. Sometimes we want to wait until we feel more equipped and better trained. Other times, we become hesitant even to the point of avoidance. If we are going to accomplish great things for God, sometimes we simply have to step out.

Joseph stepped out and God used him in the lives of two inmates when they were searching out the meaning of their dreams.

> *And they replied, "We both had dreams last night, but no one*
> *can tell us what they mean."*
> *"Interpreting dreams is God's business," Joseph replied.*
> *"Go ahead and tell me your dreams."*
> **Genesis 40:8 (NLT)**

And note here, sometimes those who should be supporting us the strongest seem to be those who withhold their support. Sometimes those who we have helped in the past simply forget what we have done for them—or they get side-tracked and lose their focus to remember.

> *Pharaoh's chief cup-bearer, however, forgot all about Joseph,*
> *never giving him another thought.*
> **Genesis 40:23 (NLT)**

The process is extremely painful when it seems like those who should be supporting you and standing with you appear to have forgotten you. The process is teaching us complete trust in God. Do you have people you have helped in the past—and it seems like they have forgotten all about that which you had done for them? Or they have turned their backs on you? Regardless of the case and of your feelings,

God can bring restitution to you, or He can choose a totally different avenue to accomplish what He wants to do in you. *Trust His process.*

Life Principle

| Proverbs 3:5-6 reminds us, *Trust the Lord with all your heart.* |

Trust in the Lord with all your heart
And do not lean on your own understanding.
In all your ways acknowledge Him,
And He will make your paths straight.
Proverbs 3:5-6 (NASB)

Trust His process; God has a way of vindicating His own. Maybe it's fleshly to say, but there is often a "sweetness" found in God's vindication.

In Joseph's case, even though his jail "friend" had made promises to Joseph and then forgot them, God still had a plan. God still had His process. And God then caused Pharaoh to have a dream.

Two full years later, Pharaoh dreamed that he was standing on
the bank of the Nile River.
Genesis 41:1 (NLT)

Mind you, this happened two years AFTER Joseph's jail friend's jailhouse promise—but God caused Joseph's "supporter" to remember to support him.

Finally, the king's chief cup-bearer spoke up. "Today I have been reminded of my failure," he told Pharaoh. "Some time ago, you were angry with the chief baker and me, and you imprisoned us in the palace of the captain of the guard. One night the chief baker and I each had a dream, and each dream had its own meaning. There was a young Hebrew man with us in the prison who was a slave of the captain of the guard. We told him our dreams, and he told us what each of our dreams meant. And everything happened just as he had predicted. I was restored to my position as cup-bearer, and the chief baker was executed and impaled on a pole."

Genesis 41:9-13 (NLT)

Life Principle

At the right time in the process (when we are ready) God will put people in place to open the door to what the process has been preparing us for. He will speak to the hearts of people, he will even change the minds of kings.
Trust the God of the process.

Because of Joseph functioning in his gifting and anointing, Joseph approached his vindication. God was clearly continuing to take Joseph through His process. This somewhat parallels the "filling" in the process of making tea: God was filling Joseph with Himself.

"It is beyond my power to do this," Joseph replied. "But God can tell you what it means and set you at ease."

Genesis 41:16 (NLT)

Life Principle

The process humbles us and teaches us that it is all about Him. He is the One with the power. He is the One with the wisdom and the knowledge. Trust Him in the process.

And so, Joseph was vindicated and given something even beyond his once-held leadership. Now, he wasn't simply the servant of Potiphar; instead, he was the "right-hand man" to Pharaoh, himself. So Joseph was vindicated—and more—for Pharaoh saw a likeness of God Himself in Joseph.

Joseph's suggestions were well received by Pharaoh and his officials. So Pharaoh asked his officials, "Can we find anyone else like this man so obviously filled with the spirit of God?" Then Pharaoh said to Joseph, "Since God has revealed the meaning of the dreams to you, clearly no one else is as intelligent or wise as you are. You will be in charge of my court, and all my people will take orders from you. Only I, sitting on my throne, will have a rank higher than yours." Pharaoh said to Joseph, "I hereby put you in charge of the entire land of Egypt."
Genesis 41:37-41 (NLT)

Life Principle

The process reveals the reflection of Jesus in us. And as others see the wisdom and intellect that is in us because of His Presence, doors will open and opportunities will be presented. Trust the process.

As God completed the process inside of Joseph, so Joseph was being catapulted into his purpose and destiny. God even used Joseph to go back and bless those who were used as a part of the process. And know this as well: **God will use you to go back and bless those who were used as part of your process.**

Life Principle

As God works His process in us, He then catapults us into the purpose and destiny for our lives. Trust the process.

And He will use the fruit of the process to restore relationships.

But don't be upset, and don't be angry with yourselves for selling me to this place. It was God who sent me here ahead of you to preserve your lives. This famine that has ravaged the land for two years will last five more years, and there will be neither plowing nor harvesting. God has sent me ahead of you to keep you and your families alive and to preserve many survivors. So it was God who sent me here, not you! And he is the one who made me an adviser to Pharaoh—the manager of his entire palace and the governor of all Egypt.
Genesis 45:5-8 (NLT)

Life Principle

It was God who sent you through the process to prepare you so that He can use you for much bigger purposes than you saw in the beginning. Trust the process.

Jim **52** Cheri

Joseph saw himself as a leader and his brothers bowing before him. Instead, God's plan was to position him to preserve many lives. This certainly was an enjoyment of that which was produced. Remember, God's plans are bigger.

For just as the heavens are higher than the earth,
so my ways are higher than your ways
and my thoughts higher than your thoughts.
Isaiah 55:9 (NLT)

Life Principle

The purpose of the process is much bigger than you can see. Stay in the process. *Trust the process.*
Trust the heart of the God of the process.

Part Four
The Creation of a Pearl

And we know that God causes everything to work together for the good of those who love God and are called according to his purpose for them.
Romans 8:28 (NLT)

So be truly glad. There is wonderful joy ahead, even though you must endure many trials for a little while. These trials will show that your faith is genuine. It is being tested as fire tests and purifies gold— though your faith is far more precious than mere gold.

1 Peter

1: 6-7 _NLT_ So when your faith remains strong through many trials, it will bring you much praise and glory and honor on the day when Jesus Christ is revealed to the whole world.

4

Pearls are rare and expensive. Other jewelry is often fashioned out of precious metals and jewels that are found buried in the Earth. But, pearls are different; they are found inside a living creature, an oyster. They are the result of a biological PROCESS—the oyster's way of protecting itself from *irritating foreign substances.*

The concept that forms the pearl is that it all begins with an irritation, a piece of sand that gets inside an oyster and just keeps irritating and irritating and irritating. As the oyster grows in size, its shell must also grow. The *mantle* is an organ of the oyster that produces the oyster's shell, using minerals from the oyster's food. The material produced by the mantle is called *nacre.*

Nacre lines the inside of the shell. The formation of a natural pearl begins when a foreign substance slips into the oyster between the mantle and the shell, which irritates the mantle.

It's kind of like the oyster getting a splinter.

The oyster's natural reaction is to cover up that irritant to protect itself. The mantle covers the irritant with layers of the same nacre substance that is used to create the shell. This eventually forms a pearl. A pearl, therefore, is a foreign substance covered with layers of nacre.

Most pearls that we see in jewelry stores are nicely round-ed objects; these are the most valuable ones. Conversely, this infers that not all pearls turn out so well.

Cultured pearls are created by the same process as natural pearls, but are given a slight nudge by pearl harvesters. To cre-ate a cultured pearl, the harvester opens the oyster shell and cuts a small slit in the mantle tissue. Small irritants are then inserted under the mantle. After much time, this process has the result of a beautiful pearl.

We all have irritants, things that really get under our skin.

- But what happens when the irritant is us?
- What happens when I am the problem—the irritant?
- What happens when personal qualitites and personality traits—even immature giftings—are the irritants?
- We need, then, to be processed.

We can see this process in the life of Peter, the disciple of Christ.

THE LIFE OF PETER

In his lifetime, Peter had many highs and lows, and certainly, many of those aspects were irritants. In fact, in many of those episodes, Peter was his own worst irritant. He was actually among the first disciples called by Jesus, and he was frequently their spokesman—for better or worse—and many of those times for the worst.

Interestingly, when Jesus told Peter, and his brother, Andrew, to "follow me," they simply <u>walked away</u> and left everything they had without even giving a second thought.

When Simon Peter realized what had happened, he fell to his knees before Jesus and said, "Oh, Lord, please leave me—I'm such a sinful man." For he was awestruck by the number of fish they had caught, as were the others with him. His partners, James and John, the sons of Zebedee, were also amazed. Jesus replied to Simon, "Don't be afraid! From now on you'll be fishing for people!" And as soon as they landed, they left everything and followed Jesus.
Luke 5:8-11 (NLT)

This meant that they left everything—all of their fishing boats, their fishing nets, and all the accessories that came with their trade. How many of us today would be willing to leave our own business to follow someone that had simply asked them to follow Him?

Peter was a fisherman, and Jesus made him a "**fisher** of **men**."

Jesus called out to them, "Come, follow me, and I will show you how to fish for people!"
Mark 1:17 (NLT)

And later, Peter was the **first** to call Jesus—the Son of the Living God—the Messiah.

Then he asked them, "But who do you say I am?" Peter replied, "You are the Messiah."
Mark 8:29 (NLT)

Remember, while we're talking about oysters and irritants, remember that there were qualities in Peter that were irritants:

- He was outspoken, and bold to a fault.
- Many times, Peter would put his foot in his mouth.
- He was quick to handle things "off the cuff" or as a "knee-jerk reaction."
- He would also just as soon cut someone's ear off as to mince words with him.
- He could also make a promise, having failed to count the costs, and then break his word.
- Peter was bold, but often, in his boldness, he was wrong.
- Once, he even rebuked the Lord.
- Another time, he said that he was willing to die for Jesus even though, shortly thereafter, at the arrest and later trial of Jesus, Peter denied Jesus three times.

*From then on Jesus began to tell his disciples plainly that it was
necessary for him to go to Jerusalem, and that he would suffer
many terrible things at the hands of the elders, the leading
priests, and the teachers of religious law. He would be killed,
but on the third day he would be raised from the dead.
But Peter took him aside and began to reprimand him for
saying such things. "Heaven forbid, Lord," he said. "This will
never happen to you!"*
Matthew 16:21-22 (NLT)

Ultimately, Peter was a sinful man.

*And this time their nets were so full of fish they began to tear!
A shout for help brought their partners in the other boat, and
soon both boats were filled with fish and on
the verge of sinking.*

When Simon Peter realized what had happened, he fell to his knees before Jesus and said, "Oh, Lord, please leave me— I'm such a sinful man."
Luke 5:6-8 (NLT)

He was also a salty, testy **fisherman**. Fishermen at that time were gruff, unkempt, vile, shabbily dressed, and often used vulgar language. Some have suggested that the fisherman of the first century was a *man's man*. This is perhaps why fishermen James and his brother John were called the *Sons of Thunder* in Mark 3:17. Theirs was a rough life, since fishing was a very physically demanding job. They must have been somewhat fearless, too, because some of the storms that came quickly upon the Sea of Galilee were fierce and furious. They often caught the fishermen by surprise and could easily capsize the 20 to 30 foot boats these men used.

THE TRANSFORMATION OF PETER

With the thought of the oyster and the pearl in mind, it was God, covering or coating Peter's irritants, that worked His process in Peter. God actually took the very things in Peter's life that were irritants and He coated them in His transformation process and they became the very <u>strengths</u> that empowered Peter to be a powerful and effective leader for the early church.

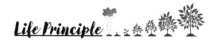

Life Principle

God will use the process of transformation to cause the very things that you struggle with to become the strengths you need to walk in His plans and purposes.

Peter was transformed by the __revelation__ of God the Father at Caesarea Philippi—and Peter voiced that statement that Jesus truly WAS the Messiah, the Son of the Living God.

Simon Peter answered, "You are the Messiah, the Son of the living God." Jesus replied, "You are blessed, Simon son of John, because my Father in heaven has revealed this to you. You did not learn this from any human being.
Matthew 16:16-17 (NLT)

Part of your process necessitates that revelation that God *is* God. He is bigger than any situation you may be facing. He is the Center of your existence and purpose. Today, these understandings do not come by study or teaching—but only through the revelation of the Holy Spirit.

Life Principle

Our transformation process includes a revelation of who He is, who we are, and of our need for Him. Trust His process.

Love is God's __expression__ of His Grace. God's grace, expressed through His love as it was to Peter, when Jesus called for him after His resurrection, is totally unmerited. It was not earned then, and it cannot be earned today. All godly transformation processes begin with God's grace and love. All transformation in us begins—not with a change on <u>our</u> parts—but with His grace on <u>His</u> part.

Life Principle

His love works in our lives like the nacre works in the oyster. It covers and coats the things we struggle with (our weaknesses), the irritants in our lives, until they become things of strength and beauty. Trust the process.

As Peter received and responded to this revelation of the Messiahship of Jesus, and as he yielded to the grace that Jesus poured out on him after the Resurrection, Peter was totally transformed by the action of the Holy Spirit.

But Peter, standing up with the eleven, lifted up his voice, and said unto them, Ye men of Judaea, and all ye that dwell at Jerusalem, be this known unto you, and hearken to my words: For these are not drunken, as ye suppose, seeing it is but the third hour of the day. But this is that which was spoken by the prophet Joel; And it shall come to pass in the last days, saith God, I will pour out of my Spirit upon all flesh: and your sons and your daughters shall prophesy, and your young men shall see visions, and your old men shall dream dreams: And on my servants and on my handmaidens I will pour out in those days of my Spirit; and they shall prophesy:
Acts 2:14-18 (KJV)

And there were miraculous results from Peter's divinely inspired proclamation.

> *Then they that gladly received his word were baptized: and the same day there were added unto them about three thousand souls.*
> Acts 2:41 (KJV)

Peter, the erratic and irritant disciple, became the **first individual** to preach on the day of Pentecost after the coming of the Holy Spirit. He also became the first one to proclaim Jesus as the *Messiah—the Christ to the Gentiles*—specifically, Cornelius and his household, in Acts 10 and 11. His transformation changed him so much that he—in latter years—**willingly** suffered persecution, imprisonment, beatings, and even verbally rejoiced in the fact that he was worthy to suffer disgrace for the Lord's sake.

> *The apostles left the high council rejoicing that God had counted them worthy to suffer disgrace for the name of Jesus.*
> Acts 5:41 (NLT)

Notice that the very things *that earlier* were "irritants" in Peter's life and influence, had now—**because of his transformation**—become his strengths because of the process.

Life Principle

The very things that are "irritants" in us become strengths throughout, and because of, the process.
Trust the heart of God in the process.

And what does Peter have to say about the process he went through, and through which you and I go through?

[You should] be exceedingly glad on this account, though now for a little while you may be distressed by trials and suffer temptations, So that [the genuineness] of your faith may be tested, [your faith] which is infinitely more precious than the perishable gold which is tested and purified by fire. [This proving of your faith is intended] to redound to [your] praise and glory and honor when Jesus Christ (the Messiah, the Anointed One) is revealed.
1 Peter 1:6-7 (AMPCE)

In view of all this, make every effort to respond to God's promises. Supplement your faith with a generous provision of moral excellence, and moral excellence with knowledge, and knowledge with self-control, and self-control with patient endurance, and patient endurance with godliness, and godliness with brotherly affection, and brotherly affection with love for everyone. The more you grow like this, the more productive and useful you will be in your knowledge of our Lord Jesus Christ. But those who fail to develop in this way are shortsighted or blind, forgetting that they have been cleansed from their old sins.
2 Peter 1:5-9 (NLT)

The process will show the **genuineness** of our faith:

- In the process... add to your faith *moral excellence*.
- In the process... add to your moral excellence *knowledge*.
- In the process... add to knowledge *self-control*.
- In the process... add to self-control *patient endurance*.

- In the process... add to patient endurance *godliness*.
- In the process... add to godliness *brotherly affection*.
- In the process.. add to brotherly affection *love for everyone*.

Life Principle

As we continue to grow through the process, we become more productive and useful in our knowledge of Jesus.

THE TRANSFORMATION OF YOU AND ME

God in His grace <u>chooses us</u> and initiates His process within us. In that process, the **irritant** becomes a *thing of beauty*. That's because God knows how to **handle** the irritants of our lives and how to <u>work</u> them as part of our transformation.

Life Principle

God takes the irritants in our lives and by His Holy Spirit... through the process... He coats them with His love, His forgiveness, and His Word and then turns those irritants into amazing pearls of strength. Trust the process.

CONCLUSION

From an arrogant, cocky, man of thunder, he became a humble, willing, obedient servant of the Lord—even unto his death. He rejoiced in the day of his death, knowing that he would be reunited with his Beloved Savior, Jesus Christ. Some scholars have estimated that his lifetime was about 65 years—of which his last 40 would be devoted to proclaiming the Gospel of Jesus Christ. It is interesting that in the Old Testament, the number 40 was considered as a number of testing—and tested, Sᴛ. Peter the Apostle, certainly was.

And he passed these tests in glorious colors... with a few retakes along the way!

This lowly, yet fiery, fisherman became a mighty *fisher of men*—and one that changed and shaped this world forever. And he is **still** proclaiming the Gospel of Jesus Christ through his influence of the Gospels, through his life and preaching in the book of Acts, and through the two general epistles that he penned: 1 Peter and 2 Peter.

Life Principle

As we submit to the process, and as we **remain** in the process, God will transform us into world changers in our world... in our sphere of influence.

Part Five
The Process of Becoming a Butterfly

Ask me and I will tell you remarkable secrets you do not know about things to come.
Jeremiah 33:3 (NLT)

If you keep quiet at a time like this, deliverance and relief for the Jews will arise from some other place,

Esther

4:14 _NLT_

but you and your relatives will die. Who knows if perhaps you were made queen for just such a time as this?

5

I LOVE THE JOURNEY (OR PROCESS) OF THE CATERPILLAR as it becomes what it is destined to be: a beautiful butterfly flying free! It is a perfect picture of the process through which we journey in order to become all that God created us to be. This journey is difficult at times, but it is in the struggle—that process—that we *become*.

There are four stages in the transformation process that gives off the beauty of a butterfly flying free.

The first stage is the **egg stage**. The female butterfly lays eggs on plants—tiny, tiny eggs. Something amazing is beginning in that small, cramped, and dark place.

The second stage of the transformation to become a butterfly is that of the **hatching stage**—from the dark, cramped egg to be a chubby, little caterpillar. My guess is that the chubby caterpillar might wonder what God was thinking when He created him—a slow moving, not-so-pretty creature that crawls around chewing on leaves—just getting fatter. But God has a plan; God has a purpose.

Then comes the **cocoon stage**. I'm pretty sure that caterpillar probably thinks life is over when it seemingly ends up all wrapped up tightly in that dark, cramped cocoon. And then its body parts completely break down into mush—a liquid state—and are reframed into the wings and the body of a beautiful butterfly. *Keep in mind, the caterpillar still can't see what God sees.*

The final stage of the transformation is possibly the hardest and the most painful. It is a time of struggle for freedom to become all that God created it to be: a beautiful butterfly. **The struggle (the process)** was required for the butterfly to emerge strong and healthy, ready to fly free, to go through all its life without any obstacles that would cripple it. That butterfly would not be as strong as it is without that struggle to be freed from the cocoon.

The process has purpose. But there is one thing different between us and the butterfly.

The butterfly goes through **metamorphosis** only once; it fulfills its purpose and then it dies.

You and I, however, go through many metamorphoses during our lifetime as He continues to complete that good work He began in us.

Let's look into the life of a young woman who, through the process, became a beautiful butterfly of grace and beauty and bravery.

For if you keep silent at this time, relief and deliverance shall arise for the Jews from elsewhere, but you and your father's house will perish. And who knows but that you have come to the kingdom for such a time as this and for this very occasion?
Esther 4:14 (AMPC)

LEARNING FROM ESTHER

In ancient Persia, King Xerxes was throwing a royal party of epic proportions! He invited all his nobles and officials, all the military officers, and princes and nobles of other provinces. **(Esther 1:1-3)**

The celebration lasted 180 days—a tremendous display of the opulent wealth of his empire and the pomp and splendor of his majesty.
Esther 1:4 (NLT)

When that was over the king threw another party—this time for all the people in Susa—from the greatest to the least. It lasted seven days! It was held in the courtyard of the palace garden and the description of the decor was amazing. **(Esther 1:4-5)**

The courtyard was beautifully decorated with white cotton curtains and blue hangings, which were fastened with white linen cords and purple ribbons to silver rings embedded in marble pillars. Gold and silver couches stood on a mosaic pavement of porphyry, marble, mother-of-pearl, and other costly stones. Esther 1:6 (NLT)

Beautifully and individually, uniquely-designed golden goblets were used to serve a seemingly endless supply of the royal wine, reflecting the king's generosity. **(Esther 1:7)**

At the same time, Xerxes' wife, Queen Vashti was giving a banquet for the women in the royal palace. (Esther 1:7-9)

On the seventh day of the feast, when King Xerxes was in high spirits because of the wine, he told the seven eunuchs who attended him—Mehuman, Biztha, Harbona, Bigtha, Abagtha, Zethar, and Carcas— to bring Queen Vashti to him with the royal crown on her head. He wanted the nobles and all the other men to gaze on her beauty, for she was a very beautiful woman. But when they conveyed the king's order to Queen Vashti, she refused to come. This made the king furious, and he burned with anger. He immediately consulted with his wise advisers, who knew all the Persian laws and customs, for he always asked their advice.
Esther 1:10-13 (NLT)

To make a long story a little shorter, because of her refusal to come at the King's request, Queen Vashti was forever banished from the presence of King Xerxes, and he was to choose another queen more worthy than she.

After the king's anger subsided, he regretted his decision and he missed his queen. I picture him being in the *mulligrubs!* I'm sure he was driving his personal attendants crazy, so they sought out something to make the king happy again.

Let us search the empire to find beautiful young virgins for the king. Let the king appoint agents in each province to bring these beautiful young women into the royal harem at the fortress of Susa. Hegai, the king's eunuch in charge of the harem, will see that they are all given beauty treatments. After

that, the young woman who most pleases the king will be made queen instead of Vashti." This advice was very appealing to the king, so he put the plan into effect.
Esther 2:2b-4 (NLT)

The king loved their idea, so he put the plan into action and all the beautiful, young virgins were brought in to Susa for the king's pleasure.

This all opened the door to a beautiful, young girl named Hadassah (her Hebrew name), who was also called Esther (her Persian name). Her parents had died and she was being raised by her kinsman, Mordecai. Thus begins the process to prepare her for her destiny.

THE PROCESS

Esther was taken from her place of love and security, and comfort. I can imagine she was scared and disillusioned.

As a result of the king's decree, Esther, along with many other young women, was brought to the king's harem at the fortress of Susa and placed in Hegai's care.
Esther 2:8 (NLT)

Esther was loved and cared for by her "kinsman", Mordechai. He (and others) taught her God's Word and raised her to live a life that honored God. But now, Esther was taken from life as she knew it, and really had no choice in the matter.

Although the Old Testament really does not give a whole lot of detail here, there were obviously sexual advances made by

King Xerxes toward Esther, even if Esther was, as the rabbis say, unwilling. However, even in all the apparent "wrongness" of what was happening to Esther, God was not absent—He had a plan.

Life Principle

There are times that we are pulled from the life we know and love. We have no choice in what is happening. Even in the midst of all the "wrongness," God is not absent—He has a plan. We need to trust His process; to trust the heart of the God of the process.

Remember, Kinsman Mordechai had reared Esther to be faithful to the Torah and all of its Laws. He had made sure that she was taught in the Word of God as much as a young girl was allowed to be taught. She was intended to live a life true to the Lord. But now, Esther was put in a place that defied all that she was.

Before each young woman was taken to the king's bed, she was given the prescribed twelve months of beauty treatments—six months with oil of myrrh, followed by six months with special perfumes and ointments. When it was time for her to go to the king's palace, she was given her choice of whatever clothing or jewelry she wanted to take from the harem. That evening she was taken to the king's private rooms, and the next morning she was brought to the second harem, where the king's wives lived. There she would be under the care of Shaashgaz, the king's eunuch in charge of the concubines. She would never go to the king again unless he had especially enjoyed her and requested her by name.
Esther 2:12-14 (NLT)

At the King's command, Esther found herself in:

- a place that did not worship the one true God
- a place that would not honor her purity
- a place that would require her purity from her

Yet, even in this "Godless" place, Esther's God never walked out on her. He was there preparing the place—and the people—for his "queen" to be positioned for the salvation of His people. He was preparing Esther for her destiny.

Life Principle

You may be in a "Godless" place—but God has NOT walked out on you. You may not see it, but He is preparing the place and the people needed for you to be positioned for the salvation of many. He is preparing you for your destiny. *Trust the process.*

An important observation to be made is that even when we are pressed out of our comfort zone—even into forced ungodliness, those qualities of character that we developed under the power of the Holy Spirit and the awesome care of Godly leaders will—somehow—shine through. For Esther, those instilled Godly qualities brought her favor—even in the "Godless" place where she did not deserve, nor did she want to be.

Hegai was very impressed with Esther and treated her kindly. He quickly ordered a special menu for her and provided her with beau-

ty treatments. He also assigned her seven maids specially chosen from the king's palace, and he moved her and her maids into the best place in the harem.

Esther 2:9 (NLT)

Esther's character and beauty impressed a very important person, Hegai. She was favored. He treated her kindly and he gave her the best of everything in order to prepare her to find favor with the king.

Life Principle

No matter where you find yourself, maintain that Godly character and allow your God-given gifts to shine. God will use your character and your gifts to gain you favor with important people who will put things into place to open doors to God opportunities and destiny.
Trust the process.

Esther also exhibited the character of listening carefully. She not only listened to, but she followed the Godly advice of those who had responsibilities for and in her. Even contrasting the claims that are often made concerning teen-agers listening to the advice and guidance of their elders,
Esther listened to, and obeyed Mordecai, her kinsman.

Esther had not told anyone of her nationality and family background, because Mordecai had directed her not to do so.

Every day Mordecai would take a walk near the courtyard of
the harem to find out about Esther and what
was happening to her.
Esther 2:10-11 (NLT)

 She listened to Hegai, her caregiver.

When it was Esther's turn to go to the king, she accepted the
advice of Hegai, the eunuch in charge of the harem. She asked
for nothing except what he suggested, and she was admired by
everyone who saw her.
Esther 2:15b (NLT)

Listening to and following their advice brought great
favor and positioned her for God's purposes.

Life Principle

While in the process, it is critical that we have wise advisers and counselors speaking into our lives. As we listen to those people God places in our lives, and as we heed their advice, it sets us up for great favor and it positions us for God's purposes—even when we don't know what those purposes are. Even then, trust the process.

Esther walked in the grace and beauty God gifted her with even in the midst of very difficult circumstances. Her grace and beauty immediately won the heart of the king. Some rabbis have suggested that Esther's was a supernatural beauty.

*Esther was taken to King Xerxes at the royal palace in early
winter of the seventh year of his reign. And the king loved
Esther more than any of the other young women. He was so
delighted with her that he set the royal crown on her head and
declared her queen instead of Vashti. To celebrate the occasion,
he gave a great banquet in Esther's honor for all his nobles
and officials, declaring a public holiday for the provinces and
giving generous gifts to everyone.*
Esther 2:16-18 (NLT)

King Xerxes loved Queen Esther more than any other women. The king was so delighted with her that he made her his queen. He even celebrated with a huge feast, declared a public banquet, gave generous gifts to everyone—all because he was smitten with Esther.

Life Principle

As you continue to walk through the process with the grace God has given you He will bring others into your life to love you and to be a part of positioning you for His purposes. Trust His process.

Just as God was positioning Esther for great purposes, He also was positioning others around her to assist her in accomplishing God's purposes. God was setting Esther up for success.

- He placed Hegai in her life giving her favor, wisdom and knowledge.
- He put Mordecai in a position of importance: *Even after all the young women had been transferred to the second harem and Mordecai had become a palace official..."* (Esther 2:19 NLT)

- He gave Mordecai opportunity for the king to be indebted to him. *One day as Mordecai was on duty at the king's gate, two of the king's eunuchs, Bigthana and Teresh—who were guards at the door of the king's private quarters—became angry at King Xerxes and plotted to assassinate him. But Mordecai heard about the plot and gave the information to Queen Esther. She then told the king about it and gave Mordecai credit for the report. When an investigation was made and Mordecai's story was found to be true, the two men were impaled on a sharpened pole. This was all recorded in* **The Book of the History of King Xerxes' Reign.** *(*Esther 2:21-23 NLT)
- And as she gained the love and favor of the king, it positioned her as queen—a place of power.

Life Principle

In your process, God will position people in your life that are there to impart favor, wisdom, and knowledge to you. Receive it! He will also be positioning people for your future success. Trust His process.

THE PURPOSE OF THE PROCESS

Keep in mind that Esther was no prognosticator and could not see the future that was before her. She basically had to take one day at a time and live that day out to its fullest—all without any vision for how or why God was developing her the way that He was. For Esther, the purpose of the process was to prepare and position her for the salvation of the Jewish people.

For if you remain silent at this time, relief and deliverance for the Jews will arise from another place, but you and your father's family will perish. And who knows but that you have come to your royal position for such a time as this?"
Esther 4:14 (NIV)

Esther had no idea when she was ripped from her family and put in the king's harem that it was for a great purpose. She had no idea she was actually being prepared and positioned by God Himself for the salvation of her people. But just like the caterpillar that, through the process became the amazing and beautiful creature that God created and purposed it to be, Esther emerged as a strong, confident, humble, wise, capable woman that God used to save His chosen people.

What is the process for which you are in preparation and positioning?

As we enter into the process, we probably have no idea of its purpose—or usually, even that it is taking place. In the midst of the process we don't see what God is preparing and positioning us for. But as we submit to God and to His process, we, too, will emerge like the butterfly--prepared and positioned for God's purpose and plan.

For I know the plans and thoughts that I have for you,' says the Lord, 'plans for peace and well-being and not for disaster, to give you a future and a hope.
Jeremiah 29:11 (AMP)

And who knows that perhaps, <u>you</u> are being processed—prepared and positioned—for a *such a time as this* moment?

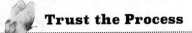

Life Principle

Trust that God has you in this process. Your process has purpose. God is using the process to prepare and position you for the very thing for which He created and destined you. For who knows but that He is positioning you for "such a time as this." *Trust the process.*
Trust the heart of the God of the process.

Esther went through her own metamorphosis as did the caterpillar. The purpose was to prepare and position her for her destiny.

God will take you and me through metamorphoses to prepare us for His destiny in our lives.

Part Six
Hope in the God of the Process

But the LORD's plans stand firm forever;
his intentions can never be shaken.
Psalm 33:11 (NLT)

Psalm

If I ride the
wings of the
morning,
if I dwell
by the
farthest oceans,

Jim **86** Cheri

139:9-10 NLT

even there your hand will guide me, and your strength will support me.

6

God the Storm Calmer

Life Principle

You are NOT in your storm alone, God—the Storm Calmer is right there with you. He was in the fiery furnace, and He was in the lion's den and He is there with you in your situation. Trust Him in the process.

JESUS CALMED THE STORMY SEA. Today, God is still that same God, the One Who calms the storms, in our lives. And we all have storms that enter our lives. Know that storms are a part of God's process in your life.

Then Jesus got into the boat and started across the lake with his disciples. Suddenly, a fierce storm struck the lake, with waves breaking into the boat. But Jesus was sleeping. The disciples went and woke him up, shouting,
"Lord, save us! We're going to drown!"

Jim **88** Cheri

Jesus responded, "Why are you afraid? You have so little faith!"
Then he got up and rebuked the wind and waves,
and suddenly there was a great calm.
The disciples were amazed. "Who is this man?" they asked.
"Even the winds and waves obey him!"
Matthew 8:23-27 (NLT)

I think we all can admit that there are many different storms in our lives.

- Job loss / Business struggles
- Marriage difficulties
- Relationship difficulties
- Health issues
- Financial problems

Many times, those storms come crashing in suddenly—when we least expect them. Although we can take certain precautions, I'm not sure we can ever fully prepare for these situations; they never come at a convenient time. At the same time, these storms always bring some kind of change with them: for good or for bad. It is at these times that a choice must be made. Depending on our final choice, we can be driven away from the Calmer of the sea, or we can be driven to Him.

In other words, we can choose how we receive these life changes. What will your response be? Many times, our responses are those of cowards or those who are faint of heart.

- Our storms can make us despondent.
- Our storms can cause us to want to give up.
- Our storms can seem undefeatable and unstoppable.
- Our storms can make us fearful.

Life Principle

We WILL experience storms in our lives. The only thing that will take us through our storms is knowing Him, really knowing Him, and being rooted firmly in His Word. Our faith must grow strong in Him. Trust His process.

And still, we must remember that there is One who is the Calmer of the storm; His name is Jesus. He has accomplished this task before. He can do it again. And we can receive Him, or reject / neglect Him, when He comes alongside of us to calm our storms.

Jesus encounters your every storm with complete confidence—He knows what He's doing.

- Your storm is no match for Him.
- Your storm does not catch Him by surprise.
- Your storm must bow before Him.
- Your confidence must *not* be in the storm.
- Your confidence *must be* in the Lord who stills the nastiest of storms.

Life Principle

The storm is simply an occurrence or phenomenon; His calming of the storm is a miracle. There is no storm too strong for Him. He is the Storm Calmer. Trust Him in the process.

So, what should you do?

- Know He is in the storm with you.
- Trust in Him, not the storm.
- Draw near to Him.
- Allow Him to do His work.
- Trust the process.

Life Principle

Keep your focus on the Storm Calmer, not the storm. Trust the process.

We should also work His Word into our lives; this gives us the foundation to stand through the storm.

"Anyone who listens to my teaching and follows it is wise, like a person who builds a house on solid rock. Though the rain comes in torrents and the floodwaters rise and the winds beat against that house, it won't collapse because it is built on bedrock. But anyone who hears my teaching and doesn't obey it is foolish, like a person who builds a house on sand. When the rains and floods come and the winds beat against that house, it will collapse with a mighty crash."
Matthew 7:24-27 (NLT)

The fears of the wicked will be fulfilled; the hopes of the godly will be granted.
Proverbs 10:24 (NLT)

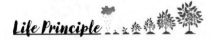

Life Principle

When the storm is over, there's nothing left of the wicked. Good people, firm on their Rock foundation, aren't even fazed. Trust the process.

And we need to step back and see and experience His victory.

Life Principle

In our storms, we too, can cry out our *whys, where are yous,* and *don't you cares.* But He is our Storm Calmer—and He is looking for our faith. Trust the process.

As evening came, Jesus said to his disciples, "Let's cross to the other side of the lake." So they took Jesus in the boat and started out, leaving the crowds behind (although other boats followed). But soon a fierce storm came up. High waves were breaking into the boat, and it began to fill with water. Jesus was sleeping at the back of the boat with his head on a cushion. The disciples woke him up, shouting, "Teacher, don't you care that we're going to drown?" When Jesus woke up, he rebuked the wind and said to the waves, "Silence! Be still!" Suddenly the wind stopped, and there was a great calm. Then he asked them, "Why are you afraid? Do you still have no faith?"
Mark 4:35-40 (NLT)

Life Principle

How do we reflect the character of God as the Storm
Calmer? We can only reflect Him as the storm calmer
if we have built our foundation on Him and His Word.
Then, we must stand in faith that He will calm our
storm. Trust Him through the process.

BA'AL PERAZIM—THE LORD OF THE BREAKTHROUGHS

*When the Philistines heard that David had been anointed king
of Israel, they mobilized all their forces to capture him. But
David was told they were coming, so he went into the strong-
hold. The Philistines arrived and spread out across the valley
of Rephaim. So David asked the Lord, "Should I go out to fight
the Philistines? Will you hand them over to me?"
The Lord replied to David, "Yes, go ahead. I will certainly
hand them over to you." So David went to Baal-perazim
and defeated the Philistines there. "The Lord did it!" David
exclaimed. "He burst through my enemies like a raging flood!"
So he named that place Baal-perazim (which means "the Lord
who bursts through"). The Philistines had abandoned their
idols there, so David and his men confiscated them.
But after a while the Philistines returned and again spread out
across the valley of Rephaim. And again David asked the Lord
what to do. "Do not attack them straight on," the Lord replied.
"Instead, circle around behind and attack them near the poplar
trees. When you hear a sound like marching feet in the tops of
the poplar trees, be on the alert! That will be the signal that
the Lord is moving ahead of you to strike down the Philistine
army." So David did what the Lord commanded, and he struck
down the Philistines all the way from
Gibeon to Gezer.*
2 Samuel 5:17-25 (NLT)

David was the newly anointed king over Israel. The Philistines were anxious to show their mighty power by defeating him and the Israelite army in battle. But King David, having heard of this, did a very wise thing that all of us need to do when we see attacks coming our way: **He sought the Lord for guidance and wisdom.**

God gave him the guidance to know that He—God—would deliver the Philistines into David's and his soldiers' hands. I love the words that the Lord had spoken to David in His instructions: "Go up, for I will certainly give the Philistines into your hand." 2 Samuel 5:19b (ESV)

David acknowledged God's promise and defeated his mortal enemies, the Philistines. And again, I love what David said when he defeated them at the place of Perazim. He said, "The Lord has broken through my enemies before me like a **breaking flood.**" And the author of 2 Samuel wrapped this conquest up with these words—and take strong note of these words with implications to soon follow: "Therefore the name of that place is called Ba'al Perazim [which means, 'Lord of the Breakthroughs'.]" 2 Samuel 5:20b (ESV)

And because of this, I present the idea to all who are reading this that God has a breakthrough for you, too.

HOLDING FAST FOR A BREAKTHROUGH

God has a breakthrough waiting on us. Even as He calmed the stormy sea, He knows where we are and has His presence ready to be with us—not only WHEREVER we are—but in whatever circumstance we may find ourselves.

Friends, to walk patiently through these times with Him, we should have trust and faith—and we get that by hearing His

Word preached, by reading His Word, and by holding on to His Word. We must hold fast to the Word of the Living Lord.

Let us hold tightly without wavering to the hope we affirm, for God can be trusted to keep his promise. Let us think of ways to motivate one another to acts of love and good works. And let us not neglect our meeting together, as some people do, but encourage one another, especially now that the day of his return is drawing near.
Hebrews 10:23-25 (NLT)

To *hold fast* presents the picture of a bulldog—one who is offered the most delicious bone he has ever seen.

- That bulldog WILL NOT let this bone go.
- He wants it with all his heart, mind, soul and strength.
- NOTHING will come between that bulldog and his bone.
- He is *tenacious*. This simply means that he holds fast to that which he has ahold of.

Let's think about the parallels we can derive from this glimpse of the bull dog.

- We are to hold tightly to the hopes and dreams that we have. We WILL NOT let go.
- We are to desire our hopes and dreams with all of our heart, mind, soul, and strength.
- We must allow NOTHING to come between us and

our dreams and hopes.
- We are to be tenacious. HOLD FAST.

In other words, don't let the enemy steal your joy, your dreams, and your identity and place in Christ. Then, you can be knocked down, but you don't have to be defeated.

We are ignored, even though we are well known. We live close to death, but we are still alive. We have been beaten, but we have not been killed.
2 Corinthians 6:9 (NLT)

- You can become perplexed, confused and discombobulated—but you don't have to stay there.
- You can become wounded and sick, but you don't have to die.

You don't have to give up your hopes and dreams—especially when knowing that the dreams that God has placed in you are for His purpose.

- One of God's purposes is to develop character in you.
- Another of God's purposes is to align you with His thoughts, ways, and patterns.
- Trust God's process.

"My thoughts are nothing like your thoughts," says the Lord. "And my ways are far beyond anything you could imagine. For just as the heavens are higher than the earth, so my ways are higher than your ways

and my thoughts higher than your thoughts.
Isaiah 55:8-9 (NLT)

- And still another of God's purposes is that His Kingdom might be increased.

ENEMIES OF OUR BREAKTHROUGH

But at the same time, we must recognize that there are enemies in our midst. Satan himself—with all of his lies—is our known enemy; his purpose is to steal, to kill, and to destroy us.

Time is a great enemy that often goes undetected. Over such time, without seeing the immediate victory, we may grow weary and forgetful. We may forget His ways, and gifts, and callings. But if we hold on to Him, and present ourselves properly before Him, we will be rewarded.

So humble yourselves under the mighty power of God, and at
the right time he will lift you up in honor.
1 Peter 5:6 (NLT)

There are also friends and family who—although they may love us and think they have our best interest in mind—But they do not understand what God is doing in us. Again, they may honestly think that they have our best in mind. And in the same thought, spiritual people may find walking by faith to be frightening—at least it is to those who are merely observing and not participating.

And you, too, can be your own worst enemy.

When defeat seems imminent, it often seems easier to succumb to that defeat rather than to fight against it. Despair and depression can cause you to be lackluster in your performance. Even tenacity can decay due to our weariness. According to *John 10:10a*, Satan's tactics can prevail: *The thief's purpose is to steal and kill and destroy...*

DETERMINE TO BE AN OVERCOMER

But it doesn't have to be that way. Determination—being willing to hold fast to the Word of the Lord—is a strong factor in being an overcomer. We just need to trust the process.

> *Let us hold tightly without wavering to the hope we affirm, for God can be trusted to keep his promise. Let us think of ways to motivate one another to acts of love and good works. And let us not neglect our meeting together, as some people do, but encourage one another, especially now that the day of his return is drawing near.*
> Hebrews 10:23-25 (NLT)

- Renew the focus, the dream, the hope.
- Tenaciously hold on to that dream of hope.
- Determine in your heart that you will not, never ever, let go of your hopes and dreams that God has planted within you.
- And hold fast to that which He has placed in you.
- Then see the victory—He is the Lord of the breakthroughs.

So David went to Baal-perazim and defeated the Philistines there. "The Lord did it!" David exclaimed. "He burst through my enemies like a raging flood!" So he named that place Baal-perazim (which means "the Lord who bursts through").
2 Samuel 5:20 (NLT)

In David's life, he saw God breakthrough for him and his people. He followed God's path explicitly—even though it was carried out differently than the previous victory had been. And because of God's Grace, and David's and his men's obedience, the victory was given. David experienced a breakthrough against the Philistines. And as you do similarly, you, too, will experience a breakthrough in your situation.

Life Principle

Lord of the breakthrough—Ba'al Perazim—which literally means "Lord of the breakthroughs." Trust the Lord of the breakthroughs in the process.

Don't let the enemy steal your joy, your dreams, and your identity and place in Christ Jesus.

Trust in the God of the Process!

Trust in the heart of the God of the Process!

Conclusion
Submit to the Process

Is anyone thirsty? Come and drink—
Isaiah 55:1a (NLT)

"Is anyone thirsty? **Come and drink**—*even if you have no money!*
Come, take your choice of wine or milk—it's all free!
Why spend your money on food that does not give you strength?
Why pay for food that does you no good?
Listen to me, and you will eat what is good.
You will enjoy the finest food.
"<u>*Come*</u> *to me with your ears wide open.*
Listen, and you will find life.
I will make an everlasting covenant with you. I will
give you all the unfailing love I promised to David.
See how I used him to display my power among the
peoples. I made him a leader among the nations.
You also will command nations you do not know,
and peoples unknown to you will come running to
obey, because I, the Lord your God, the Holy One of
Israel, have made you glorious."
Seek the Lord while you can find him.
Call on him now while he is near.
Let the wicked change their ways
and banish the very thought of doing wrong.
Let them turn to the Lord that he may have mercy on them.
Yes, turn to our God, for he will forgive generously.
"My thoughts are nothing like your thoughts," *says the Lord.*
"And my ways are far beyond anything you could imagine.
For just as the heavens are higher than the earth, so my ways
are higher than your ways and my thoughts higher than your
thoughts.
"The rain and snow come down from the heavens and stay on the
ground to water the earth. They cause the grain to grow, producing
seed for the farmer and bread for the hungry.

It is the same with my word.
I send it out, and it always produces fruit.
It will accomplish all I want it to,
and it will prosper everywhere I send it.
You will live in joy and peace.
The mountains and hills will burst into song,
and the trees of the field will clap their hands!
Where once there were thorns,
cypress trees will grow.
Where nettles grew, myrtles will sprout up.
These events will bring great
honor to the Lord's name;
they will be an everlasting sign of his
power and love."

Isaiah 55:1-13 (NLT) (emphasis added)

- Come and Drink.
- Listen and Find Life.
- Seek and Find the Lord.
- Call on Him while He is Near.

Trust the Process. Submit to the process.
Watch and see what the process works in you.

Conclusion

When we think about what the Word of God says concerning God's Process—while the words were not anything particularly new to us, they are reassuring to those of us who are in the process. Many of us have entered into a "next phase" of the process. Romans 8:28, "And we know that God causes everything to work together for the good of those who love God and are called according to his purpose for them,"—perhaps even a new process.

And we know that God causes everything to work together for
the good of those who love God and are called according to his
purpose for them.
Romans 8:28 (NLT)

His plans and purposes include us and, while primarily are for His Kingdom purpose, also include our good and our growth. And God is more concerned about our character than He is about our comfort.

For I know the plans I have for you," says the Lord.
"They are plans for good and not for disaster, to give
you a future and a hope.
Jeremiah 29:11 (NLT)

Another thought to realize is that God's knowledge does not require our understanding.

"My thoughts are nothing like your thoughts," says the Lord.
"And my ways are far beyond anything you could imagine.
For just as the heavens are higher than the earth, so my ways are
higher than your ways and my thoughts higher than your thoughts."
Isaiah 55:8-9 (NLT)

 Some of us stop growing—we stagnate—because we feel that we need to understand in order to proceed. But we need to stop trying to understand everything—especially the thoughts of God and His ways.

Don't worry about anything; instead, pray about everything.
Tell God what you need, and thank him for all he has done.
Then you will experience God's peace, which exceeds anything
we can understand. His peace will guard your hearts and
minds as you live in Christ Jesus.
Philippians 4:6-7 (NLT)

- Don't worry about anything
- Pray about everything
- Tell God what you need
- Thank Him for all He has done

Then...

You will experience God's peace... more than you can even understand. That peace will take up guard in your heart and mind as you live in Him.

In fact, we CANNOT comprehend God in His fullness; we are only granted this knowledge in part. Instead, we are simply to trust in Him. To trust His process.

Trust in the Lord with all your heart; do not depend on your own understanding. Seek his will in all you do, and he will show you which path to take.
Proverbs 3:5-6 (NLT)

God can and will use the attacks of the enemy, the bad choices that you and I and others make—and the general circumstances of life—in order to carry out His process.

We can believe this because God's ways and purposes are sure.

This God—his way is perfect;
the word of the Lord proves true;
Psalm 18:30a (ESV)

And God ALWAYS takes what the enemy intends for our harm and <u>He turns it into good</u>.

But Joseph replied, "Don't be afraid of me. Am I God, that I can punish you? You intended to harm me, but God intended it all for good. He brought me to this position so I could save the lives of many people.
Genesis 50:19-20 (NLT)

So what are we to do?

- STOP trying to figure it all out, or to second guess the process.
- STOP reaching back for the past and the comfortable.

— 💬 —

Getting over a painful experience is much like crossing monkey bars. You have to let go at some point in order to move forward.
C.S. Lewis

- GO AHEAD and grieve over it; grief is a natural response for awhile.

— 💬 —

"When you have lost something precious (your job, your house, your health, a loved one), you may think it is irrational to be joyful. But this is a worldly way of thinking. Major losses are very painful, and they do need to be grieved. Nonetheless, with time and effort you can learn to focus on the good things that remain—and find joy in the One who will never leave you."
Young, S. (2004). Jesus Today. HarperCollins.

In everything we do, we show that we are true ministers of God. We patiently endure troubles and hardships and calamities of every kind. Our hearts ache, but we always have joy. We are poor, but we give spiritual riches to others. We own nothing, and yet we have everything.
2 Corinthians 6:4,10 (NLT)

- REST assured in His promises.
- SUBMIT to the process.

And now, dear brothers and sisters, one final thing. Fix your thoughts on what is true, and honorable, and right, and pure, and lovely, and admirable. Think about things that are excellent and worthy of praise. Keep putting into practice all you learned and received from me—everything you heard from me and saw me doing. Then the God of peace will be with you.
Philippians 4:8-9 (NLT)

Change your thinking. Trust the process.
Trust the God of the process.
Trust the heart of the God of the process.

LIFE QUESTIONS

Can you trust Him?

Can you trust His process in you?

What is your level of need?

What is the largeness of your God?

What is His level of trustworthiness?

Will you trust Him?

Will you continue to trust the processes God is working in you?

Your name, O Lord, endures forever;
your fame, O Lord, is known to every generation.
For the Lord will give justice to his people
and have compassion on his servants.
The idols of the nations are merely things of silver and gold,
shaped by human hands.
They have mouths but cannot speak,
and eyes but cannot see.
They have ears but cannot hear,
and mouths but cannot breathe.
And those who make idols are just like them,
as are all who trust in them.
O Israel, praise the Lord!
O priests—descendants of Aaron—praise the Lord!
O Levites, praise the Lord!
All you who fear the Lord, praise the Lord!
Psalm 135:13-20 (NLT)

Trust the Process

Trust the God of the Process

About Jim & Cheri Garrett

Dr. James Garrett

Rev. Dr. Jim Garrett is a lover of God, the husband to one wife, the dad to three children, and the Papa to 15 grandchildren.

He hails from the great state of South Carolina, where he lived out all of his early days at the foothills of the mountains near Greenville.

He has many academic achievements including multiple degrees and awards, but his greatest reward is simply being a faithful husband, Dad, and Papa.

Jim and Cheri have been children's, youth, family pastors, lead pastors, worship leaders, and missionaries. Jim also serves as a college / seminary professor.

His joy is found in serving God by serving the Church, teaching his students, and spending time with his family and dogs.

Jim's greatest thrill in life is witnessing his next generation—his grandchildren—as they, too, grow up serving the Lord in various capacities.

He is a content man.

CHERI GARRETT

CHERI GARRETT GREW UP IN THE FOOTHILLS OF THE MOUNTAINS in a small, cotton-mill town in South Carolina.

She met Jesus at a young age when a church reached out to the children of the town by picking them up in a large, old, school bus that the church had painted purple and white. Cheri was one of the kids that rode that bus, changing the whole trajectory of her life.

Cheri married her high school sweetheart, Jim, and entered the life of "a pastor's wife" at a young age. They've been married a very long time, and still, Jim is the love of her life and her very best friend. Their legacy is their three children, three children-in-love, and 15 grandchildren, which bring Cheri and Jim so much joy and laughter... God's best blessings.

Cheri currently co-pastors Hope Church in Plain City, Ohio, alongside Jim. She has a heart for encouraging and equipping women, and is a beloved speaker in her church as well as women's events both in the states and abroad.

Cheri's favorite times are with her family. She loves yardwork in the spring and hosting guests anytime.

Cheri and Jim love doing mission work as a team, especially by encouraging and equipping pastors and their spouses. They love traveling together wherever the road, plane, or boat carries them, and hope these will continue to lead them on many other great adventures.

Our Prayer for YOU

Lord,

Thank you for allowing us the privilege of communicating these truths to every person who reads this book. These stories and illustrations are truths that you have revealed to us and that we have walked through *in the processes.* You have taught us to trust—and now, we pray that you will use what you have taught us to encourage others to trust the processes you have put in their lives— that we will all know that the processes are for your best in our lives, and they are transforming each of us day by day...

Please use these truths to increase the confidence of your people in you and your promises. Use them to challenge your people to be patient, but willing, with what you are doing in their lives... to *trust YOU in the processes.* And use them to remind your people that—as we wait on you—we will be called, empowered, transformed, and fruitful in doing what you have for us to do.

In Jesus' name, we ask these things.
Amen.

Thank you for choosing
our **Trust the Process** book and
allowing us to share some of the processes
that God has brought us through!

We pray that you are blessed
for choosing to
Trust the God of the Process!

Please consider leaving a review on the platform of purchase!
In doing so, you are graciously helping us to share
God's goodness and much needed love.
For more information about us (Jim and Cheri):
FB @Still Becoming
email: cheri@stillbecoming.net
jim@stillbecoming.net

Made in the USA
Columbia, SC
26 June 2024

37390084R00078